Puffers & Pla...

Guthrie Hutton

G. & G. Hamilton's first *Invercloy* heading west through Crinan Bridge.

Formerly Ross & Marshall's *Skylight*, *Sitka* is seen here in her guise as the *Vital Spark* in 1973.

© Guthrie Hutton, 2018
First published in the United Kingdom, 2018,
by Stenlake Publishing Ltd.
www.stenlake.co.uk
ISBN 978-1-84033-822-5

The publishers regret that they cannot supply
copies of any pictures featured in this book.

Printed by
Blissetts, West Cross Industrial Park, Brentford, TW8 9EX

Further Reading

The following were the principal books and web sites used by author during his research. None are available from Stenlake Publishing; please contact your local bookshop, reference library or search for them on the internet.

Bowman, A. I., *Kirkintilloch Shipbuilding*, 1983.
Burrows, George W., *Puffer Ahoy*, 1983.
Black, Bill, *The Glasgow Canal Shipbuilders*, (research paper) 2000.
McCallum, May F., *Spartan: Scottish Maritime Museum Collection*, 2000.
McDonald, Dan, *The Clyde Puffer*, 1977 (+ reprints).
McGinn, Keith, *Last of the Puffermen*, 2007.
Moir, Peter, & Crawford, Ian, *Argyll Shipwrecks*, 1994.
Paterson, Len, *The Light in the Glens*, 1996.

Web Sites

puffersandvics.org
clydeships.co.uk
vic27.co.uk

Acknowledgements

This is the second selection of pictures of puffers that I have compiled and again a number have come from the camera and collection of Dan McDonald, whose splendid volume, *The Clyde Puffer* remains the definitive work on these boats. I am grateful to the Ballast Trust for agreeing to their use, on pages 4, 18, 26, 27, 29, 32, 34, 40 and 44. I am likewise grateful to David Warrillow for the use of pictures from his collection, on pages 10 and 11. I must also thank the Science and Society Picture Library, © National Railway Museum, for the use of the picture on Page 17.

Introduction

'Sleek', 'graceful', 'majestic' are just some of the words that people use to describe ships, but not puffers; small, functional, unglamorous boats that would have passed into history un-noticed had it not been for the fictional exploits of Para Handy, his rackety crew and their noble craft the *Vital Spark*. She was launched in 1905 as a series of articles, in the pages of a Glasgow newspaper, the *Evening News,* written by author Neil Munro under his pen name Hugh Foulis. For many people these delightful stories are all they have ever known about puffers, they have become part of the West of Scotland's social culture and, assembled in a number of editions have never been out of print. The *Vital Spark* has also had a significant screen presence as the inspiration for a classic Ealing Comedy film, *The Maggie* and in television comedy programmes. BBC Scotland first put her on screen in 1959/60 with a series entitled *Para Handy – Master Mariner*, with one of Scotland's great comic actors, Duncan MacRae in the title role. Known as a pantomime dame and for telling the story of a 'Wee Cock Sparra', he also appeared in *Highland Voyage*, a short film made on board a puffer in 1963. Two years later a pilot programme, the *Vital Spark*, was made for *Comedy Playhouse*, the BBC's testing ground for new situation comedies. It led to two series' of programmes made in black and white, a colour series and a one-off special. A fourth series was made in 1994.

Filled with humour, the stories bear echoes of real life incidents, but there was another side to the puffer man's life. It was hard and could be dangerous, many boats were lost, and tragically men were sometimes lost with them. Like floating trucks, the boats carried goods to wherever the customer wanted. Few destinations had dockside facilities, so the puffers' ability to load and unload with their own gear was a key feature, as was being to take the ground on a receding tide. Tides and the availability of cargoes governed the puffer man's life; it was emphatically not a nine-to-five job.

Superseding sailing craft and canal barges, puffers played a vital role for over 100 years supplying remote communities and servicing larger ships, but their world began to diminish as shipping practises changed. The unkindest cut of all was the unequal struggle of trying to compete with heavily subsidised road transport. New roads, new roll-on, roll-off ferries and new ferry terminals, all built with public funds, hastened the demise of these little ships. If the puffers really were floating trucks, they and their more modern diesel counterparts were driven from the seas by trucks on wheels.

No longer braving hostile elements, these characterful boats have nevertheless left an undying legacy. The Para Handy stories live on, cafés, pubs and alcoholic beverages are named after them, a couple of boats have been kept as museum exhibits and enthusiasts strive to keep others afloat. The puffer has thus joined the roster of maritime legends, not a single great ship, but a fond memory filled with good cheer.

The Advance, with a small puffer half-hidden alongside, at East Bay, Dunoon some time prior to 1910.

Filming is a time-consuming and expensive activity so it is standard practice in the industry to work with a main production unit and a second unit filming minor scenes. For *The Maggie* this meant two identical puffers and the boats that landed these starring roles were the *Boer* and *Inca*, two 72 ton coastal vessels belonging to J. Hay and Sons Ltd. Built in 1941, *Boer* was the younger of the two, *Inca* was three years older. She is seen above in her normal guise and left sporting her film name, *Maggie*, in the Crinan Canal, one of the film's principal locations. Another film industry practice is to do all of the production work under a working title, allowing the final name to emerge from the process. The working title for *The Maggie* was *Highland Fling* – well the puffer's crew did lead the wealthy American, Calvin B. Marshall and his hapless agent, a merry dance! A book telling the story of *The Maggie* was published in 1954 to coincide with the launch of the film.

Transmitted early in 1966 the first series of six *Vital Spark* programmes was mainly studio based, but with filmed inserts shot on location with the *Saxon*, a puffer owned and operated by Walter Kerr of Millport. He was proud of his boat, so he cleaned her up for the telly, only for a scenic artist to splash dirty paint on her to make her look 'authentic'. She is seen here at Inveraray and Brodick looking suitably grubby. Built by J. & J. Hay in 1903 and originally named *Dane*, *Saxon* got her new name in 1914 when she was upgraded for coastal work. She sank off Gourock in 1925 following a collision with the Belfast collier *Melissa*. She was bought where she lay by Finlay Kerr who, with his son Walter raised her and put her to work trading between Millport and the mainland. A familiar sight on the Clyde for 40 years, she had reached the end of her working life when the BBC hired her for one last hurrah! As the *Vital Spark* she was crewed by Roddy MacMillan as Para Handy, Walter Carr as Dougie the mate, John Grieve as MacPhail the engineer and Alex MacAvoy the cabin boy Sunny Jim. They were a wonderful cast.

The same cast featured in a second black and white series of the *Vital Spark* produced in 1967. *Saxon* had gone to the breaker's yard so a new boat, the *Starlight*, was cast in the title role. Seen here at Rothesay, she was built for the Greenock-based company Ross & Marshall in 1937, but soon after the filming finished she too went to the breaker's yard. Colour television had arrived by 1973 when a special hour-long programme was made to mark BBC Scotland's 50th anniversary. The next year some of the earlier programmes were remade as a colour series. By this time few steam puffers remained and the boat used was the *Sitka*, formerly Ross & Marshall's *Skylight*, a near sister of *Starlight* built in 1935. She had an undignified end, sinking beside the wall of Bowling Harbour before being taken over to Gourock where attempts to restore her failed before she too was scrapped.

The Vital Spark sailed again in 1994 with a new series, *Tales of Para Handy* and an entirely new cast headed by Gregor Fisher as Para. The boat used for the series was the *Auld Reekie,* an Admiralty fleet tender formerly known as *VIC 27*. She got the new name, with its Edinburgh associations and allusions to the boat's smoky lum, courtesy of Sir James Miller, the former Lord Provost of Edinburgh and Lord Mayor of London. He bought the boat in 1967 and converted her for use as a training vessel for youth clubs. She was sold in 1979 and taken to Crinan where for a few years she was hired out to holidaymakers and spent the summer of 1988 as part of a Para Handy themed exhibit at the Glasgow Garden Festival. After starring as the real thing, she languished at Crinan before being taken over by a group of enthusiasts. They began an ambitious restoration project, and *Auld Reekie* got on the telly again when their endeavours were featured in a series for BBC Alba. She is seen here in her youth club role at Fort William Pier.

The Kerr family's cargo carrying business, which ended with the *Saxon's* stint as the *Vital Spark* in 1965, began almost 100 years earlier when Walter Kerr realised he could make more money trading than by fishing. He began by using his fishing boat and had earned enough by 1880 to commission a new sailing smack from Fife's boatyard at Fairlie. Named *Jessie Kerr* she is seen here (on the left) at Millport. A few years later a second smack named *Mary Kerr* was commissioned from Fife's boatyard. Initially skippered by Walter's son John, she was later sold to a new owner based at Lochranza on Arran where, sitting on the beach in front of the distinctive castle, she can be seen discharging a cargo. The boat was eventually wrecked at Brodick in 1927. The *Jessie Kerr* was also wrecked, on Horse Island at Ardrossan Harbour in 1913, but undaunted her skipper, Walter's other son Finlay replaced her with a yawl from the East Coast and then the steam driven *Saxon*.

Sailing vessels like the *Mary Kerr* and *Jessie Kerr* were typical of the kind of craft that predated steam power. They carried all those unglamorous commodities like coal, sand and bricks usually associated with puffers, on trading routes around the Clyde estuary and West Coast. They also served major industries like the slate quarries of Easdale and Ballachulish. Various types or rigs of craft were employed, including cutters, ketches, sloops, smacks or yawls, but most appear to have been known by the single word: 'gabbart'. This splendid picture taken in 1893 shows one such boat powering along under full sail and described in an accompanying hand-written note as a 'collier on the Clyde'. It seems somehow counter-cultural to see such grace and elegance deployed on the every day carriage of a humble cargo like coal, but that's how it was and it was boats like these that the puffers supplanted.

Although paddle steamers had been plying the Clyde since 1812 when Henry Bell's *Comet* first took to the water, the birthplace of the puffer wasn't the river, but the Forth & Clyde Canal. Steam propulsion was first seen on the canal in 1803 when William Symington conducted trials of his paddle steamer *Charlotte Dundas*. They were successful, but despite that a nervous canal company halted further trials and subsequent attempts to introduce steam made little impact. By mid century, with trade being lost to the railways, the canal proprietors realised that something had to be done. The answer came with screw propulsion, a development that had been attracting interest from shipping companies for almost ten years before 1856 when the canal company agreed to have the lighter *Thomas* converted at Hamilton Hill in Glasgow. With a boiler and engine mounted aft she will have looked very similar to this steam-powered lighter photographed at Ruchill in the late 19th century.

The successful conversion of the *Thomas* prompted other lighter owners to follow suit and in 1857 the *Glasgow*, a new steam-powered, iron-hulled lighter of 60 tons was launched onto the canal at Kelvin Dock. Regarded as the first puffer, she is one of many vessels built at Kelvin Dock. Situated between Locks 22 and 23, it formed part of a heroic construction completed between 1785 and 1790 that included five locks and the great Kelvin Aqueduct. Incorporated into the boatyard was a superb dry dock that could be drained into a lower basin through a culvert. The area was initially named Port Kelvin, but also became known as 'the dock', 'the dry dock' or 'Kelvin Dock', until more land from the Garscube Estate was needed to accommodate the growing village. This was granted on condition that it 'shall be in all times called the town of Mary Hill'. Mary, who had inherited the estate from her father Hew Hill, was thus immortalised. The distinctive but now demolished Maryhill Cross buildings are seen here behind the *Onward* just after her launch in March 1910.

Kelvin Dock was operated by a number of tenants, but the one whose name became almost synonymous with it was David Swan who took over in 1836. It was in his time that the *Glasgow* was built. David Swan was also a pillar of local society and became Maryhill's first provost when it gained Police Burgh status in 1856. The Swan family's interest in the dock ended in 1889 when William Swan retired and passed the business on to his brother-in-law William Marshall. A new owner, Richard Munro, took over in 1910. The *Hafton* was launched in that year and she is thought to be the boat seen in this picture emerging from the sea lock at the western end of the Crinan Canal about 1913. She passed through the canal again in September 1933 bound for Mull with a load of coal, but crossing the Firth of Lorne sprang a leak and sank. The crew fired flares and sounded the horn, but there was no response, so they took to their small boat and saved themselves.

The *Effort* was another product of Kelvin Dock. She is seen here at Hunters Quay, on the left-hand edge of the picture alongside the *Advance*, which is also in the picture on page 3. There is something almost heroic about these little steamers bearing thrusting, dynamic names like *Forward*, *Advance* and *Effort*. Launched in 1884 for James McCreath and Charles Hendry of Hunter's Quay, *Effort* was bought by J & E McNeill of Greenock in 1905. She was stranded between Kilcreggan and Cove in January 1927 and became a total loss. Hunters Quay, just to the north of Dunoon, was a natural puffer haven but its place in the annals of Clyde shipping was secured in June 1973 when Western Ferries selected it as the terminal for their new ferry crossing from McInroy's Point. The service was put on in competition with the established, subsidised MacBrayne's ferry route between Gourock and Dunoon.

Like the *Effort*, *Sunflower* was launched at Kelvin Dock in 1884. Seen here at Oban, she traded widely on the West Coast of Scotland and Northern Ireland, but her final ten years were spent working on the Mersey where she foundered in 1920. It wasn't the first time she was wrecked. That happened on the Antrim coast in 1890, although she was subsequently salvaged. Before and after that incident, she had a number of owners, although the poster offering her for sale in 1896 did no favours by misprinting her building date as 1844 instead of 1884.

Porpoise, on the left, and *Mallard* were for much of their existence in the fleet of Glasgow Steam Coasters Ltd. managed by the firm of Paton and Hendry whose name appears on the sale notice for *Sunflower* on the facing page. One of the partners, John M. Paton surprised the puffer world in 1911 when he ordered a number of motor vessels, but to the relief of steam traditionalists the technology proved unreliable, stifling an innovation that could have transformed the puffer trade long before owners started to install diesel engines in their boats. A traditional steam puffer, *Porpoise* was built on the Forth & Clyde Canal in 1893 at Hamilton Hill and was heading east on the canal through Lock 37 at Old Kilpatrick when this picture was taken. *Mallard* was a younger boat having been built in 1902 by Scott & Son at Bowling. She is seen here beside the little jetty at Salen on Loch Sunart in Ardgour.

People tend to think of puffers solely as West Coast boats, but some did cross over to the east and a few were built for East Coast owners. One of these, the 73 ton *John Strachan*, seen here in a picture of Kirkcaldy Harbour, was built at Kelvin Dock in 1885 for the Kirkcaldy, Leith and Glasgow Steam Packet Company, but taken over in 1890 by another Kirkcaldy-based owner. One significant cargo carried from the east to the west was barley, for use in distilleries and the *John Strachan* is thought to have been engaged in this trade when she went aground at Ardbeg, Islay in December 1917. She became a total loss.

Some East Coast boats were familiar sights on the Forth & Clyde Canal, most notably the sizeable fleet of lighters operated by the Carron Company. The Carron Iron Works went into blast on Boxing Day 1760. It was huge then and grew to become one of the dominant Scottish industrial concerns with, not just the massive ironworks but a fleet of ships based on Grangemouth. Their lighters didn't have names, only numbers, as is clear from this picture of No. 5 tied up on the towpath side at Ruchill. The Craighall Works of the Kelvin Chemical Company was to the right of where the boat is sitting, with access off the towpath. On the offside, behind No. 5 are the Ruchill Iron Works and Alexander Fergusson & Coy's Glasgow Lead and Colour Works. Heavily polluting industries like these, and MacLellan's Rubber Works just to the east of Ruchill Bridge were established at Ruchill in the latter years of the 19th century when there was no room for further development at other canalside locations like Port Dundas.

Another East Coast operator whose lighters were a familiar sight on the canal was Christian Salvesen of Leith and Grangemouth. One of the company's boats, the *Comet*, built by Scott and Sons of Bowling in 1882, is seen here in Bowling Basin. From the outset the heaviest trade on the canal was between the Grangemouth Docks and Hamilton Hill in Glasgow, and this increased after 1790 when the extension to Port Dundas was opened. When steam lighters were developed they supplanted the heavy horse-drawn lighters and the trade continued. Such was the volume that Port Dundas was, in part at least, an extension of the Grangemouth Docks, with its wharves bearing East Coast names like Carron, Leith, London and Kirkcaldy – even Hamburg! On the outbreak of the First World War commercial traffic in the Forth above Rosyth was stopped, isolating Grangemouth and the canal. The lighters, including eight belonging to Salvesen stopped working.

The East Coast also featured in the story of *Ina Mactavish*. Built at Hamilton Hill in 1886 for Angus Mactavish of Ardrishaig, she sank twenty years later, but was raised, repaired and lengthened. She was bought by owner/skipper John Wilson of Leith who left South Shields with lime for Aberdeen on 16th October 1907 (the picture is incorrectly dated). During the night the condenser broke down and eight hours later the engine stopped. Steering with a sail, Wilson beached just north of the Northumbrian coaling port of Amble. The local coastguard teams were quickly on the scene, but the exhausted crew were unable to attach lines and the Alnmouth lifeboat, delayed by dithering and confusion, took six hours to reach them. In that time the engineer was washed overboard and the young cook died of exposure. It was not the RNLI's finest hour. The ship was later re-floated: a loose nut had caused the condenser problem and a rope wrapped around the propeller stopped the engine. Amble folk were no strangers to maritime tragedy, but this one, played out in slow motion, caused particular distress in the town.

The *Rachel* was built on the canal at Hamilton Hill in 1892 for James Burrows. He kept her in immaculate condition, but because she was comparatively small he replaced her within a few years with a larger boat, the *Petrel,* ordered from the Larne Shipbuilding Company in Northern Ireland. *Rachel* was almost certainly under new ownership when this undated picture of her was taken and used as a postcard with the title 'Timber Boat, Holy Loch'. She has been drawn up on the beach at Sandbank, with the anchor in the foreground. To the left two figures are silhouetted against the surface of the loch; there is a horse, a cart of sorts and a splash as a log is tipped into the water to be floated across to the boat. It was a clever way of loading heavy timber. This industrial activity is in marked contrast to the steam yacht, a symbol of conspicuous wealth, sitting out in the loch behind the puffer.

Another Hamilton Hill product was the *Glenfinart*, seen here beside the jetty at Inveraray. Built in 1892 she was owned by a consortium of fishermen from Ardentinny for most of her working life, but that ended about 1926, which helps to date the picture. To enthusiasts of the *Para Handy* stories, Inveraray is a special place, Neil Munro's home town. He was born at Crombie's Land, close to the imposing courthouse, was buried in Kilmalieu Cemetery on Loch Fyneside and is commemorated in Glenaray by a monument overlooking his family's ancestral home village. Also, much of the filming for the early *Vital Spark* programmes involving the *Saxon* and *Starlight* was done at Inveraray, with some of the activities of the real puffer crews easily matching the fictional tales being acted out for the camera. The historic burgh is seen here from the main pier with crowds of people, presumably steamer passengers heading into town along the old stone jetty.

The popular image of the puffer is of the boat sitting on a beach unloading her cargo onto carts. It sounds simple, perhaps with a hint of romance, but it was neither of those things. Puffers had a keel and were broad, beamy little boats, but not flat-bottomed and landing on a beach was potentially hazardous because a stray rock could damage the hull, so boat owners and crew kept careful notes on which beaches were safe. One commodity often delivered this way was coal, a tough cargo for the men to dig through at the best of times, but doubly back breaking when having to be done before the boat floated on the next tide. The boat in this picture is the *Zephon*, which was built in 1901 by Scott and Sons of Bowling and acquired by J. & J. Hay of Kirkintilloch in 1922. The company appears to have kept her name despite adopting a practice in the late 19th century of giving their boats warrior or tribal names. *Zephon* was an angel battling with Satan in John Milton's epic poem *Paradise Lost* – perhaps fighting with the devil was warlike enough!

J. & J. Hay bought the *Macnab* from her original owners, W. H. King, but unlike *Zephon* she was given a new identity: *Spartan*, the first of three boats to bear a name that became one of the best known in puffer annals. Built on the canal at Hamilton Hill in 1893, *Spartan* (1) is seen here to the west of the Temple Locks in a picture that appears to have been taken shortly after her acquisition by Hay's in 1901. On the left are piles of fireclay pipes, the product of the Garscube Brick and Tile (or later Brick and Pipe) Works. On the other side of the canal is timber stacked in the yard of Robinson Dunn's Temple Sawmills: timber was one of the main commodities carried on the canal, with large quantities imported through Grangemouth. Looking past the puffer's bow, in the background is the railway bridge over the minor road that led to Netherton Farm and Bridge. Hay's sold *Spartan* (1) in 1923, but three years later bought the *Tiree* and renamed her *Spartan*. This second boat to bear the name blew up and sank off Lismore in 1946 while still on Government service following the Second World War. A third *Spartan* joined the fleet soon after (see page 30).

Canalside boatyards in Glasgow may have pioneered the conversion of canal lighters to steam power and then building prototype puffers, but the place that became most closely identified with puffers, perhaps even their spiritual home, was Kirkintilloch. Situated almost mid-way between the East and West Coasts, this inland town might seem an unlikely spot for such an activity, but it flourished thanks to the brothers James and John Hay. For some years, their father William, a Kirkintilloch man, had operated a fleet of lighters on the canal, based at Port Dundas. Facilities for repair and maintenance were few, so in 1867 the brothers took over a small boatyard, which had been started only a year earlier just to the west of the Townhead Bridge. As business grew J. & J. Hay began to build new boats and to launch them side on into the canal. This was quite a spectacle as the launch of the *Tuscan* in 1934 shows – the company, by this time styled J. Hay & Sons Ltd. even used the picture as an advertising card.

FROM J. HAY & SONS LIMITED,
45 RENFIELD STREET,
GLASGOW, C.2.

TELEPHONES
CENTRAL 8331-4
(4 LINES).

TELEGRAMS—
STEAMER DEPT.—"HAYSTRATH." GLASGOW.
LIGHTER DEPT.—"HAY."   DO.
ALSO AT GRANGEMOUTH.

Launch from J. Hay & Sons Limited's boatyard on 21st November, 1934, of s.s. "TUSCAN" (140 tons)—the fifty-fourth vessel built and engined by them for their near-coasting trades.

The men at J. & J. Hay's Townhead yard built good boats, a tradition established by the de facto yard manager John Thom and continued by his son George. These men didn't work to drawings, only by eye, allied to skill and experience. The quality of their work can be gauged from this picture taken inside the hold of the *Saxon*, over 60 years after her launch (as the *Dane* in 1903). In that time this somewhat battered space had been on the receiving end of innumerable loads of coal tipped into it from a great height. The boat had also absorbed the impact of a collision and immersion in the Clyde for a few months. Although the sunk *Saxon* was not raised by J. & J. Hay the firm did have a squad of men who were expert in salvaging boats that had come to grief. Strandings, sinkings and other potentially terminal incidents happened surprisingly often and equally often the boats were able to sail another day thanks to the quality of Kinkintilloch workmanship.

Lock Nos. 33-36 on the Forth & Clyde Canal, known collectively as the Boghouse Flight were at different times flanked by brickworks. The Garscadden Brick and Tile Works was beside Lock 34 on the south bank of the canal, while a later works was set up to the north of the canal at Drumchapel by one of the country's largest brick and tile manufacturers Peter and Mark Hurll. A tramway ran from it to a loading point on the canal at the tail of Lock 36. Market and supply fluctuations periodically affected output, but puffers were still loading bricks here in the 1930s as this picture of the *Serb* shows. Launched by J. Hay and Sons Ltd. in 1927, she was the second boat to bear the name, her predecessor having been stranded and wrecked off Ardbeg on Islay in December 1925. She was sold in 1958 to John Dutch & Son of Perth who used old boats to dredge sand from the River Tay. That company was taken over in 1963 by Earnbank Sand and Gravel Ltd who promptly scrapped all of the old steam vessels, although *Serb* (2), renamed *Foam*, may have gone to the breakers before that.

As canal-built puffers ventured further from the flat calm of the waterway, they were adapted to cope with different and more testing conditions. Three broad types of vessel emerged, so-called 'inside boats', suited only for work on the canal or Grangemouth Docks, 'shorehead boats', adapted to operate in the relatively benign waters of the Clyde before it widens out into open water and 'outside, or coastal boats' equipped with hatch coamings and covers for the heavier conditions of the Firth of Clyde and beyond. One of these 'outside' boats was the *Cuban* of J. Hay & Sons Ltd., built at Kirkintilloch in 1935. Unlike the *Serb* on the facing page she has a wheelhouse, a later concession to the comfort of the helmsman who, on older boats had to stand out in all weathers with only a canvas dodger for protection. *Cuban*, seen here on the Clyde passing Dumbuck was broken up in 1960.

Although the puffers originated on the Forth & Clyde Canal, they became such a familiar sight on the Crinan Canal that they are more popularly associated with it, a perception reinforced by the *Maggie's* rackety passage through the canal. The boat navigating the canal here in a more orderly fashion is the *Cretan* of J. Hay and Sons Ltd., which is going through the Dunardry Locks, No. 11 (left) and No. 10 (right). Boats like the *Cretan* that were built on the Forth & Clyde Canal, had no problem with the Crinan's locks, which were about twenty feet longer, wider by two feet and a foot or so deeper. Some bigger puffers were built to Crinan Canal dimensions, although one owner, who allowed for a slight misalignment of Lock 11, discovered the hard way that the cill of Lock 5 at Cairnbaan was larger than the others. Launched in December 1939 *Cretan* sank off Rothesay in 1954, but was raised and continued in service until 1965 – not long after these pictures were probably taken.

At 99 tons the *Ardfern* was bigger than the *Cretan*, but not too big for the Crinan Canal. She was also built at Kirkintilloch on the Forth & Clyde, but not at Hay's Townhead Yard. She was a product of the Canal Basin Yard operated by the town's other boat builder, Peter McGregor & Sons. She is seen here manoeuvring to enter Lock 8 at Cairnbaan at the eastern end of the Crinan's summit pound, 1,114 yards long and 64 feet above sea level. Although only nine miles long, the canal was a boon to small ships like puffers. It was made as a short cut between the Clyde estuary and the Firth of Lorne, and as a way for fishing boats and other craft to avoid the long and hazardous passage round the Kintyre Peninsula. The locks are numbered from east to west, with the sea lock at Ardrishaig being No. 1 and the western sea lock at Crinan being No. 15. Built in 1910 for Glasgow-based owners, *Ardfern* was later sold to the Warnock brothers of Paisley who operated a large fleet of lighters. She was scrapped in 1966.

In 1939, just before the Second World War, Scott & Sons of Bowling built two boats named *Anzac* and *Lascar* for J. Hay & Sons. They were as long, wide and deep as the Forth & Clyde Canal could accommodate, but their shape and size also proved ideal for the Admiralty, which adopted the design during the Second World War for a large number of fleet tenders known as Victualing Inshore Craft or VICs. Originally identified with numbers, not names, these boats were largely the products of English boatyards, but two were built at Kirkinitilloch. One of them, which was launched in 1944, proved surplus to Admiralty requirements and instead went into the Hay's fleet named *Kaffir*. Originally steam-powered, she is seen here at Brodick some time after 1962 when she was converted to diesel. She came to an inglorious end in 1974 when the engineer got above his station and set sail from Ayr without the skipper or mate aboard, and ran the boat aground at the harbour entrance.

These pictures are a bit fuzzy compared to some on preceding pages, and Glasgow's urban fringe is perhaps less attractive than West Highland scenery, but there is a value to these images that transcends all that. They show *Spartan* (3), which was built at Kirkintilloch as *VIC 18* and came into Hay's fleet after the war as replacement for *Spartan* (2), lost on Admiralty service. She is seen here squeezing through Lock 31 on the Forth & Clyde Canal, with Drumchapel in the background. Begun in the early 1950s, the housing scheme's development coincided with the canal's decline and it was closed soon after these pictures were taken. Locks 31 and 32 were filled in, but the setback was not as final as it first appeared because work to reinstate the canal began in March 1999, with a formal ceremony held at Lock 31. *Spartan* (3) also had a second life. Converted to diesel in 1961, she continued to work, latterly as part of Glenlight Shipping until being withdrawn in 1980. She was sold for £1 in 1982 and has since been preserved as an exhibit at the Scottish Maritime Museum in Irvine.

The *Norman* was launched at Kirkintilloch for J. & J. Hay in 1895. She was chartered to the Admiralty during the First World War, returned to the Hay fleet and was sold in 1930 to the Arran Shipping Company. They worked her for five years before she was sold again to George Halliday of Rothesay, where this photograph was taken in 1951. Two years later the *Norman* was scrapped, but bigger changes were afoot in the puffer world. In 1956 J. Hay & Sons' coastal ships were taken over by one of the UK's largest coastal fleet owners, F. T. Everard & Sons Ltd. The puffers were moved into a new company J. & J. Hay Ltd., which joined with another operator, Hamilton & McPhail in 1963 to form a new company, Hay-Hamilton Ltd. That firm in turn joined forces in 1974 with the Greenock-based Ross & Marshall to form a management entity, Glenlight Shipping. Two years later Hay-Hamilton withdrew from the business, leaving *Spartan* as the only vessel from the original Hay fleet still operational until her withdrawal in 1980.

Another J. & J. Hay boat that was sold after about 30 years of service was the 69ton *Roman*. Launched at Kirkintilloch in January 1904, she was bought by the Arran Shipping Company in 1935 and is seen here in their colours letting off steam from the winch while unloading cargo at Brodick jetty. Sitting at the pier in the background is the British Transport Commission's cargo steamer *Kildonan*. Her presence helps to date the picture to the 1950s: built in 1933 as the *Arran*, she was renamed *Kildonan* in 1952 and withdrawn in 1957. She was like a great big puffer, with a large hold amidships and machinery aft. The crew of J. & J. Hay's *Tuscan* had reason to be grateful that she was sitting at the pier in 1955 when their boat was swamped by stormy seas, as the skipper attempted to get into Brodick with a cargo of coal. Seeing that the puffermen were in trouble, the crew of *Kildonan* came to their rescue. Both *Roman* and *Kildonan* were broken up in 1958.

When Glenlight Shipping was formed in 1974 it brought together the two largest companies still operating puffers, J. & J. Hay Ltd. and Ross & Marshall of Greenock, a company that had been formed in 1872 and over the years owned a significant number of boats. As the name implies the company was an amalgamation: Thomas Ross was in the coal trade, while James Marshall was in dock and haulage work, but they both operated lighters and this became their core business. Greenock was the ideal place from which to operate lighters either as tenders for large ocean-going ships, or as a base from which to service the needs of coastal communities. Ross & Marshall boats were easily identified by their names; they all ended in 'light', as in *Raylight* or a variation like, *Mellite* or as here the *Acolyte* of 1885. Although slightly blurred, the picture shows the minimal protection for the helmsman offered by a canvas dodger before wheelhouses were fitted to these little boats.

Ross & Marshall boats were a familiar sight alongside the pier at Portree on the Isle of Skye. The boat seen here, the *Sealight* was built by George Brown of Greenock in 1930. With dimensions tailored to suit the Crinan Canal, she was a big puffer, 85 feet in length, 19 feet 6 inches in the beam and drawing just over 9 feet. She was one of three boats to bear the name; the first was in service from 1895 to 1930, while the third *Sealight*, a coaster bought in 1988 by Glenlight Shipping and renamed, had a short and inglorious career. In the background, to the left, is David MacBrayne's diesel-electric ship *Lochnevis*. Built by Denny's Shipyard at Dumbarton and launched in May 1934, she was intended for the Malliag, Kyle and Portree mail service, with accommodation for cargo and day passengers.

Puffers are usually associated with the Forth & Clyde or Crinan Canals, but from time to time they also used the Caledonian Canal as this picture of the Fort Augustus locks shows. The 'Caley' is significantly larger than the two smaller canals so the two puffers were able to share this lock with room to spare. The people in the foreground are working one of the old style lock gate capstans; each gate was connected by chains to two capstans, one opened the gate; the other closed it. The holidaymaker who took the picture recorded the date in their photo album as August/September 1939, a significant date because war was declared on 3rd September and that may explain why the puffers were heading north. Their names are not known, but the funnel of the boat in front is clearly that of a Ross & Marshall boat. It could be *Sealight* and the other boat, with an equally distinctive funnel, could be *Glencloy*. Both worked as fleet tenders at Scapa Flow during the war and would have travelled through the canal to get there.

In an earlier era, Ross & Marshall boats were handily placed to act as tenders to various fleet configurations of naval ships moored off Lamlash on the east coast of Arran. Protected by Holy Island, Lamlash Bay was an excellent sheltered anchorage, which gave the warships ready access from the Firth of Clyde to meet any threat in the North Atlantic. The navy had long gone by the time a photographer chanced on this more peaceable scene at Lamlash, with the *Skylight* languishing at the pier. The date of the picture is not known, but it appears to have been taken in the 1950s, before cheap foreign travel lured visitors away from the Clyde Coast resorts. On this occasion Lamlash had attracted a good number of holidaymakers who are evidently enjoying one of those magical sunny days playing on the beach, building sandcastles or messing about in boats. They appear undeterred by the presence of a working puffer; perhaps without her the picture would be incomplete, for them and the photographer.

Ross & Marshall boats were easily distinguished by the funnel colour: red with a narrow black band, broader white band and a black top, divisions that are clear in this picture of *Starlight* at Paisley Harbour. The existence of a harbour at Paisley, which was latterly a Ross & Marshall fiefdom, comes as a surprise to many people. It was situated on the White Cart River about two miles south of its confluence with the Clyde. The river was navigable by small vessels, and was also viable as a base for small shipyards like that of Fleming and Ferguson, which gained a reputation for building dredgers. The White Cart navigation was made possible by the impressive bascule bridge at Inchinnan erected in 1923 by Sir William Arrol. The M8 motorway also crossed the river on a high level bridge specially built, at some expense, to allow ships to pass up to Paisley, but as it opened the harbour closed – oops!

Grounded, listing and evidently in trouble a boat is seen here beside Gourock Pier with two Ross & Marshall puffers alongside. The stricken vessel was the *Hornby*, a tug from Liverpool, which had just hauled an Italian barque to Greenock. Job done, she was returning to the Mersey, when just after midnight on 23rd March 1907 she was in collision with David MacBrayne's coaster *Handa*. The tug began taking in water rapidly, so her skipper, Captain Chadwick turned his damaged boat for the shore. She was sinking as she hit the beach. Meanwhile Captain MacKellar on the *Handa*, her bows smashed, beached stern first in Cardwell Bay to the east of the pier. Her cargo was discharged, which lightened her bows and she was able to go up river to Greenock. The puffers will have come down from Greenock to Gourock where they appear to be preparing a salvage operation, an activity that Ross & Marshall specialised in.

The second of four boats to be named *Polarlight* was built in Yorkshire during the Second World War as Admiralty fleet tender *VIC 26*. Acquired by Ross & Marshall after the war, she is seen here in the 1950s beside the Bowling Basin coal hoist. Coal trucks arrived at the hoist along the railway line that occupied the narrow strip of ground between the canal and the Clyde. Goods traffic going to and from Bowling Harbour bypassed the hoist and crossed the canal on a swing bridge set at ground level while a few yards upstream an impressive high level swing bridge took mainline rail traffic over the water. Bowling was just one coal-loading facility on the Clyde. There were others at General Terminus Quay, Queen's Dock, Princess Dock and Rothesay Dock. At some of these locations a crane lifted loaded railway trucks and tipped their contents directly into boats, a practice that also created clouds of coal dust; at others a hoist raised the truck bodily before emptying its contents onto a chute (as at Bowling) and into the hold, again generating great black clouds of coal dust.

Ross & Marshall made some modifications to the traditional steam puffer shape in 1957 with their new vessel, *Stormlight*. Like some of the wartime VIC boats she was built in Cheshire at the Northwich yard of W. J. Yarwood & Sons Ltd. At 88 feet in length, 21 feet beam and drawing nearly ten feet, she pushed the Crinan Canal dimensions to the maximum. Her hatch, 35 feet long by 14 feet wide gave access to a hold of 8,600 cubic feet capacity. She was initially powered by a steam engine, but converted to diesel in 1969. Crew accommodation was markedly different from older boats with the skipper, engineer and mate each having a separate cabin and the crew sharing a twin berth. The wheelhouse was placed forward of the funnel and the space taken up below decks for the crew allowed the lifeboat to be stowed on the poop deck abaft the funnel, an arrangement that freed the crew from having to carry the boat on the hatch covers and lift it off and on every time they needed access to the hold.

The puffers' domain spread from the canal out across the West Coast, so it is little wonder that an island like Arran should feature in their story, not just as a trading place but also as the base of one of the better-known operators, G. & G. Hamilton. Continuing a family business, brothers George and Gavin Hamilton and their father built a wooden-hulled steam lighter at Brodick in 1895 and named her *Glencloy* after one of Arran's famed beauty spots, They worked her hard and in 1904 took delivery of *Invercloy*, a new steel-hulled boat built by the Larne Shipbuilding Company in Northern Ireland. The old *Glencloy* was sold in 1911 when the *Rivercloy* joined the fleet and in 1930 a new *Glencloy* was built at the yard of Scott and Sons at Bowling. She spent the war years as a fleet tender at Scapa Flow and is seen here back on civilian duties in 1950 at Brodick's stone jetty. It sat at the mouth of the Strathwhillan Burn – the bridge carrying the road over the burn can be seen on the extreme left of the picture, with one of the island's prime hostelries, the Douglas Hotel just behind.

Puffermen preferred the jetty at Brodick as it formed a safe harbour and was cheaper to use than the main pier. In this picture, almost certainly taken at the same time as the one on the facing page, the jetty is seen with *Glencloy* alongside and Arran's most distinctive scenic feature, the 2,856 foot high mountain Goat Fell, behind. Two years before this picture was taken G. & G. Hamilton amalgamated with another small company, that of Colin McPhail whose boat names ended in 'shira', like *Stronshira* or *Glenshira*. The new company was known as Hamilton-McPhail and it continued in operation until amalgamation with J. & J. Hay Limited in 1963 to form Hay-Hamilton, one of the constituent parts of Glenlight Shipping. Built to Crinan Canal dimensions, *Glencloy*, with her tall funnel and almost elegant lines was the epitome of a puffer, but she was converted to oil burning in 1955, with a stubby funnel set behind the wheelhouse. Sold in 1966, she was stranded a year later at Cove in Loch Long and subsequently lost.

The demise of the steam puffer was signalled in 1953 when Scott and Sons of Bowling launched the diesel-powered *Glenshira* for Hamilton-McPhail. With the machinery taking up less space, the crew could be accommodated aft, but in other respects she retained traditional puffer features and carried the usual cargoes, like coal. She is seen here in Troon Harbour, which was built as a coal trans-shipment port in the early 19th century by the Duke of Portland. He not only built the port, but also constructed Scotland's first public railway, the Kilmarnock and Troon Railway, to get the coal mined on his Kilmarnock estates down to the port and onto ships. As Ayrshire's coal industry grew through the 19th century Troon, along with Ardrossan, Ayr and Girvan became major outlets, sending shiploads of coal out to West Coast communities and over to Ireland. The coal trucks seen here behind the *Glenshira* show that when the picture was taken in 1960, Troon was still exporting coal, with much of it leaving the port in the holds of puffers.

The ancient fortress of Dumbarton Rock is unmistakeable in the background of this picture showing *Dorothy* at the quay on the River Leven. Tricky to navigate, the fast-flowing river was also prone to flooding – in February 1856 a combination of tide, wind and spate resulted in the quay being overtopped by five feet. Despite the difficulties, Dumbarton folk turned the river to their advantage and gained a reputation for shipbuilding dominated by one name: Denny. Family members had been involved in shipbuilding on the river for some time before the firm of Denny Brothers was set up in 1844, and superseded five years later by William Denny and Brothers. Along with its associated engine works, the company built many fine and famous vessels, although a couple of forays into puffers were not wholly successful; there was clearly an art to puffer design! *Dorothy* was built on the canal in 1901 at Burrell's Hamilton Hill yard and was photographed in the Denny heartland in 1938.

The *Elizabeth* was built at Port Glasgow in 1866, but was owned and operated by Rothesay timber merchant George Halliday and is consequently more often associated with Bute. She is seen here at Port Bannatyne with a string of carts lined up on the quay to receive whatever cargo is being unloaded – the use of a bucket suggests it was coal. Bute was royal property when the Stuart kings were on the throne of Scotland and their chamberlains, the Bannatyne family lived at nearby Kames Castle: Port Bannatyne was named after them. Behind the children playing on the seaweed strewn shore is a fishing boat bearing the registration letters RO for Rothesay. Displaying a registration number was a legal requirement for fishing boats from 1860, with most ports of registry identified with the first and last letters of their name like CN for Campbeltown, but there are variations like BA for Ballantrae and RO for Rothesay, to distinguish its boats from those registered RY from Ramsey on the Isle of Man.

Built by A. & J. Inglis at Pointhouse in 1866, *Dunlop* was relatively old when photographed in 1905 at the slate island of Easdale. Slate quarrying was one of the biggest West Coast industries generating puffer cargoes. There were two main centres, Ballachulish and the islands of Seil, Easdale, Luing and Belnahua. At Ballachulish, boats were able to load from the beach until a harbour built of slate waste was completed, but after the railway opened in 1903 sea borne cargoes diminished. For the islands, the only practical way to transport the slate was by sea. With the exception of Belnahua, they were part of the vast estates owned by the Earl of Breadalbane and had been partially worked before 1745 when he set up the Marble and Slate Company of Netherlorn. Marble extraction was quickly abandoned, but slate quarrying continued for over a hundred years before the workings were leased to a succession of operators who kept going until just prior to the First World War. The venerable *Dunlop*, having shipped many loads of slate off the islands, was scrapped in 1922.

Of all the islands that puffers frequented, Islay with its many distilleries was one of the most important. What made the distilleries important (apart from the obvious) was that they were industries and generally needed the boat to carry an outbound load of coal, empty barrels or other supplies and return with a cargo of nectar-filled barrels. Over time, many puffers were engaged in this trade, but one, the *Pibroch* was owned by one of the distillers – White Horse – and operated solely on their business. Built by Scott and Sons of Bowling in 1923 she was replaced by a diesel coaster of the same name, also built by Scotts in 1956. The old steam *Pibroch* was sold the following year, but something of her old haunts was retained when she was renamed *Texa* after a small island off the distillery-rich south coast of Islay. She kept her new name despite a further change of owner in 1960, but when sold again in 1964 was renamed *Cumbrae Lass* after another island. She made her final trip to Arnott Young's breaker's yard at Dalmuir in 1967.